Would You Rather Family Edition

BRAIN TRAINER

How To Play ...

1) Have two or more people around (the more the better).

2) The person holding the book asks the question and the person listening HAS to answer one of the two options (no skipping).

3) Take turns asking questions (don't keep the book to yourself).

4) That's it, have fun!

Get a paper cut every day for the next month OR Bite your tongue every day for the next month?

Be trapped in a seven year old's body for the rest of your life OR In a seventy year old's body?

Would You Rather...

Have an elephant the size of a puppy OR A puppy the size of an elephant?

Be in a medieval sword fight on horseback OR In a sumo wrestling match against Asashoryu Akinori?

Do one hundred squats, pushups and crunches OR Crawl a mile on the beach like a crab?

Change your last name to Sprinkles OR Your first name to Pringles?

Accidentally dye all your clothes purple OR Your hair purple?

Be a pilot who unfortunately lost his sight OR A vet who became allergic to animals?

Would You Rather...

Get $100,000 and lose half your looks OR Get $1,000 and double your attractiveness?

Sleep in a bed without a pillow OR On the floor with ten pillows?

Work at a carnival running a hot dog stand OR Running a can shooting game?

Sit next to someone at the dinner table who keeps stealing your food OR Across from someone who talks with their mouth full?

Would You Rather...

Have free unlimited music on demand with no ads OR Unlimited movies with no ads?

____

Drive to see the world's tallest man OR The end of a rainbow?

Play a solo piano recital in a large and packed auditorium OR Be part of a street jazz band in a crowded park?

Live as a caveman among mammoths OR As Nemo among sharks?

Ride a camel across a vast desert OR Drive in a dune buggy?

Lose something you worked really hard for by following the rules OR Win by cheating?

Make the most money at a Christmas bake sale OR Get the prize for the most delicious pie?

Live near a forest inhabited by wild bears OR Live near a beach inhabited by sea lions?

Pop a balloon everytime you wanted to yell at someone OR Take a shower every time you felt like crying?

Have hands like Captain Hook OR Hands like Edward Scissorhands?

Answer your front door to find a singing telegram OR The Grinch holding a plate of your favorite cookies?

Live in a world where you rule over everyone and have complete power OR Live in a world where there are no problems?

Live in a country that was hot and rainy year round OR Cold and sunny year round?

Have super sensitive taste buds so you can experience good food even better OR A lack of taste buds so bad/healthy food is easier to eat?

Trek through a snowy forest to cut down your own Christmas tree OR To see wild reindeer?

Walk around with a single eye glass, a mustache and a pipe like a detective OR An eye patch, a peg leg and a monkey on your shoulder like a pirate?

Have hair that is always perfect OR Hair that never gets wet?

Only eat burgers from the day before for the rest of your life OR Only ever eat frozen pizza?

Be 50% more attractive OR
Increase your IQ by 50
points?

Have a lot of good friends
but also a few enemies OR
A few really great friends
and no enemies?

Create a piece of art that the world loves but get no credit OR Be the best artist in the world but no one knows you?

Give up cheese OR All dairy products but cheese?

Be a traditional belly dancing Lebanese dancer OR A Gypsie living in the 1400s?

Wear Christmas themed hats all year round OR Socks?

Be famous worldwide for living alone on an isolated island OR Live in a crowded city where nobody knows you?

Get your tongue stuck to an ice cube OR Burn it accidentally with hot chocolate?

Never age past ten years old and see all your friends get older OR Age twice as fast as everyone else?

Give the Grinch a perm OR Give Rudolph a bath?

Would You Rather...

Faint whenever you heard a car honk OR Whenever you smelled something good?

Be the most popular kid at school for misbehavior OR The smartest but not popular at all?

Be able to see into the short term future OR Be able to read your parents' minds?

Stop to help someone who fell and miss your bus OR Cause someone to fall by running to catch the bus and not miss it?

Have the highest IQ in the world OR The bank account with the most digits?

Play real life Jumanji OR Play a Jenga game with blocks the size of bricks?

Have it all OR Know it all?

Be handcuffed to a dangerous criminal OR Tied to a tree during a tornado?

Have a white and cold Christmas OR A hot and sunny one?

Never be able to stop smiling even during sad moments OR Never be able to smile at all?

Get a paper cut every time you unwrap a present OR Sit and watch someone else unwrap your presents?

Talk like Siri OR Move like C-3PO from Star Wars?

Live ten lives of fifty years each OR Live five lives of hundred years each?

Make your brother/sister do all your chores but have to eat their portion of vegetables OR Do all your brother's/sister's homework and get to choose what they wear to school?

Get transported to a world that is ugly but safe OR A world where everything is beautiful but there are many dangerous animals?

Lose all your possessions OR Have to give your pet away?

Live three separate lives simultaneously at one point in time OR Get to choose to live two extra lives at any point in history?

Be responsible for saving the world from a plague of killer bees OR From a giant asteroid?

Eat while doing a headstand OR Do your homework in a squatting position?

Demonstrate a dangerous science experiment on stage in front of thousands of people OR A safe experiment in a basement with a mad scientist?

Always answer your phone by yelling Merry Christmas OR By whispering Happy Holidays?

Win the lottery tomorrow but die next year OR Find true love tomorrow and get to live five more years?

Be able to watch your next night dreams on TV OR Be able to read people's minds any time?

Accidentally be hit in the face with a basketball by your favorite player OR Get purposefully hit in the face by your brother/sister with a stuffed animal?

Not be able to have a hot meal again OR Never have a hot shower again?

Be admired by many people you don't know OR Be admired by everyone you do know?

The person you like dates your enemy OR One of your best friends?

Go to a party of someone famous and accidentally knock over their Christmas tree OR Accidentally spill cranberry sauce all over their shirt?

Watch a one hour live music performance OR A one hour hilarious comedy stand up?

Receive a puppy as a gift OR A yearly pass ticket to the zoo?

Get your exercise dressing up like Rocky and running up stairs OR Dressing up like a ninja and doing karate?

Write a cookbook with one hundred peanut recipes OR one hundred coconut recipes?

Send Santa Claus your wish list by phone and get to talk to him OR Have a Skype call with the Grinch?

Never learn from your mistakes OR Always be too afraid to try new things?

Would You Rather...

Be really good at math but bad at English OR Really good at English and bad at math?

Have the job of creating new languages for movies OR Designing the costumes?

Would You Rather...

Live a month without sunlight OR A month without darkness?

Have someone find out you returned all the gifts they gave you OR Find out someone returned all the gifts you gave them?

Wear heavy, metal, tap dancing shoes everywhere OR A silver, sequinned tiara everywhere?

Be born with a great amount of confidence OR Into a succesful and rich family?

Give up Christmas movies OR Christmas sweets?

Pretend that you really liked a dish of mustard-soaked brussel sprouts your aunty made and eat a whole plate of it OR Pretend you had the flu and not eat anything, hurting her feelings?

Have one good friend turn up to your birthday or ten average friends show up?

Cancel Christmas and only go to school for three days a week OR Have an extra month off for Christmas but go to school every Saturday too?

Be abducted by aliens that like to have dance parties OR Abducted by chimpanzees who have secret tea parties at night?

Live within walking distance of your favorite restaurant OR Your best friend's house?

Find a valuable treasure in someone else's yard sale OR Have your own yard sale and make a ton of money at your own yard sale?

Be the assistant for a magic show with David Copperfield OR An assistant for an archeology team that just discovered a new dinosaur fossil?

Be stuck inside of an elevator for two days OR On a ski lift for two days?

Only be able to use your right hand OR Only be able to walk using one leg?

Climb 1,000 stairs to the top of a mountain with an incredible view OR Hike through the jungle to an ancient hidden city?

Sleep fully clothed in all your winter clothes OR Go out in the snow in your pajamas?

Find a tooth in your mashed potatoes OR Booger in your sweet potatoes?

Give up your bed to visiting relatives and have to sleep on the sofa OR Shower after everyone else when all the hot water is gone?

Roam around town wearing a giant astronaut helmet OR A Mexican sombrero?

Go back in time and take something out of history OR Go back and add something to it?

Be able to tell when someone's lied to you OR Be able to lie yourself out of any situation?

Miss Christmas morning by helping someone find their lost dog OR By helping your elderly neighbor clear snow from the driveway?

Would You Rather...

Be a stand-up comedian in front of a crowd of minions OR A musician in front of a crowd of dancing lemurs?

A hug from your favorite person every day for the rest of your life OR Be able to talk to animals?

Would You Rather...

Give up all drinks except water OR All foods except lasagna?

Be the main characters in Jurassic Park OR Hunger Games?

Take a selfie with a penguin wearing a Santa hat OR With a baby seal wearing a Santa hat?

Win $100,000 OR Let your best friend win a million?

Bring back all the extinct animal and plant species OR Bring back your favorite TV shows that have been cancelled?

Be a bus driver and get to talk to all the passengers OR Be a truck driver and not have to talk to anyone?

Would You Rather...

Be able to play every instrument elegantly OR Be able to speak every language in the world fluently?

Be the president of your country and make things the way you want it OR Be your favorite superhero?

Be part of a large family with mostly quiet, reserved people OR A small family with loud, outspoken people?

Wake up and realize that you overslept and missed your exams to pass the year OR You overslept and missed half your birthday?

Would You Rather...

Have three brothers OR
Three sisters?

Watch a Harry Potter
marathon OR A Star Wars
marathon?

Brush your teeth with peppermint and chocolate flavored toothpaste OR With eggnog flavored toothpaste?

Spend quality time with one person you care about on your birthday OR Attend an extravagant Christmas party with a bunch of strangers?

Watch a very scary movie alone at home OR A hilarious comedy with people continuously talking and interrupting?

Have one wish right now (no wishing for more wishes) OR Three in three years?

Do it and regret it OR Not do it and regret it?

Only wear red and green the whole month of December OR Have to sing Jingle Bells every day in front of the class?

Would You Rather...

The ability to be able to stop time for an hour a day OR Be able to rewind thirty seconds into the past?

Go shopping in an empty mall but can only take three things OR Go shopping on the busiest day of the year and get everything you fit in your cart for free ?

Only shower at 5am for the rest of your life OR Only at 11pm?

Get locked out of your car on a rainy day OR Get locked out of your house at night?

Be dressed as a character from Lord of the Rings for Halloween OR Someone from Star Trek?

Be a world class swimmer and hate the water OR A world class sprinter but hate running?

Only be able to shout for the rest of the year OR Whisper?

Create snow that glows in the dark OR Cookies that are sugar-free and good for you?

Be grounded from and not be able to play with your friends OR Not be able to play video games?

The ability to fly an hour at a time OR The ability to breathe under water for an hour at a time?

Start a successful business OR A successful religion?

Pick a charades card that read: "getting your gloves stuck in your jacket zipper" OR "Pretending to like the socks your grandpa gave you"?

Try to ask someone for directions who doesn't speak the same language as you OR Try to read a map in another language?

Have a family of white Arctic foxes living in your backyard OR A family of polar bears?

Answer thirty difficult exam questions in five hours OR Three difficult questions in five minutes?

Get food poisoning after eating your favorite food and then never want to eat it again OR Get food poisoning while on holiday?

Be known for your good looks and your fame OR Your kindness?

Eat a cone of mashed potatoes and gravy instead of ice-cream and chocolate sauce OR A bun filled with pickles inside instead of a hot dog?

The Harry Potter world be real OR The Jurassic Park world be real?

Be double your weight OR Half your height?

Be a translator for people in court OR Between a hostage negotiator and a criminal?

Help your dad wash the car and mow the lawn and skip school OR Go to school and not have to help at all?

Would You Rather...

Watch horror movies all day at school OR Romance movies all day at home?

Fall and injure your elbow so you can't use your arm OR Fall and injure your leg so you can't walk properly?

Walk backwards everyday from 1pm to 5pm OR Walk with your eyes closed after dark?

Lose your phone OR Lose your wallet?

Be given the nickname Little Cupcake OR Never be able to eat another cupcake again?

Be blind but incredibly agile with your hands OR Deaf but write the most amazing stories?

Have a baby tiger as a pet OR A sleepy monkey as a pet?

Accidentally see the Easter Bunny pooping OR The Tooth Fairy burping?

Would You Rather...

Share half of your food
with a needy family OR
Keep it all and have
leftovers for the next day?

Have a party on a plane
with amazing views OR
Party on a ship and swim in
amazing water around
you?

Admit your biggest
embarrassment on
national television OR Your
biggest mistake?

Get a bouquet of flowers
delivered to you everyday
OR A box of chocolates?

Be the president that everybody loves OR The celebrity that no one likes?

Your family baby photos get put on every box of cereal sold at the grocery store OR A recording of you singing Jingle Bell Rock gets played on the radio?

Would You Rather...

Be a wizard with magical powers OR A superhero with inhuman powers?

Enter a raffle drawing to win an electric guitar previously owned by a famous musician OR A baseball signed by a famous player?

Be a musician who slowly becomes deaf OR Be a writer who slowly loses their sight?

Learn sign language OR Braille?

Be the wittiest one out of everyone you know OR The funniest?

Work behind the scenes on a movie doing something you love OR Have a role in the movie doing something boring?

Would You Rather...

Make school holidays longer OR Candy healthier?

Operate a rollercoaster standing in the hot sun all day but get to ride it for free as many times as you want after the park is closed OR Pay and wait for one ride like everyone else?

Go without air conditioning in the summer OR Heating in the winter?

Live until one hundred fit and healthy OR Till two hundred weak and frail?

Give a speech in front of everyone you've ever known OR Dance in front of them?

Own thirty green parrots that can only say "the number you have dialed is out of service" OR Own thirty turtles that always bite your fingers?

Watch a magic show OR A performance at a circus?

Your freezer break in summer OR Your hot water system break in winter?

Would You Rather...

Eat your favorite meal for every meal for the rest of your life OR Eat it once a year but have a regular well-balanced diet?

Be diagnosed with a disease that causes you to wake up every ten minutes while you're sleeping OR A condition that causes you to cross your eyes when you become tired?

Have a personal bodyguard at all times OR A personal driver?

Have supersonic hearing so you can hear people a mile away OR Amazing vision so you can see people a mile away?

Would You Rather...

Have a family snowball fight OR Go ice-skating?

Be the star in one movie OR In one TV show with ten seasons?

Would You Rather...

Accept $100 for sure right now OR Flip a coin to win $1000?

Stand in line overnight to buy something you have always wanted that is on sale OR Stand in line for two days to buy a new item that your best friend wants for their birthday?

Have the fastest Internet in town OR Own the fastest car in town?

Do something evil for the greater good of humanity and everyone knows OR Not do it and watch the Earth deteriorate slowly?

Only have the History Channel to watch on TV OR Only have Jeopardy to watch?

Train a camel to play dead OR Train a hippo to sit?

Not be able to feel pain OR
Not be able to see colors?

Drink brown colored water
that tastes good OR Drink
clear water that tastes a bit
odd?

Go Vegan for a month OR
Only be able to eat steaks
for a month?

Go camping in the woods in
nature OR Snorkeling to
see some exotic fish?

Get to go to any island in the world for your birthday but get not presents OR Get lots of presents but stay where you are?

Understand quantum physics OR quantum computing?

Rent a bungalow on a private beach OR A cabin in the mountains?

Watch a ten minute win compilation OR A ten minute fail compilation?

Attend an Indian Wedding
and get to dress up in
colorful clothes OR
Celebrate the Chinese New
Year in China?

Live without electricity OR
Without running water?

The End

CPSIA information can be obtained
at www.ICGtesting.com
Printed in the USA
BVHW040229150920
588843BV00016B/1031

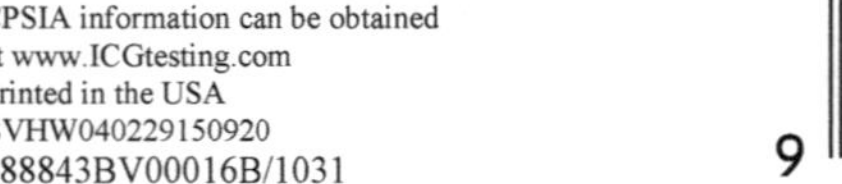